D0916942

To every young, male, BIPOC.
Always remember how powerful, intelligent, and special you are.
You can do incredible things!

To mom, dad, and granny.
The Hall Brothers are a result of your love, commitment, and hard work!

To Clay The Don.
Congratulations on your 2020 graduation!

To my Big, Little Brother.
Your work ethic and initiative is admirable! You're going big places!
- C.H.

Library of Congress Control Number: 2020918023
ISBN 978-0-578-76902-8 (hardcover) | ISBN 978-0-578-76311-8 (paperback)
ISBN 978-0-578-76312-5 (ebook)

Written, Edited & Formatted by Clamentia Hall Jr.
Cover & Interior Art by Ana Latese

First Edition

Mr. Clementine TEACH
IG: mr.clementineteach | mr.clementineteach@gmail.com | TPT: MrClementineTEACH

BROWN BOY DREAMS

CLAMENTIA HALL JR.
ILLUSTRATED BY ANA LATESE

There was a brown boy, and he had big dreams!

How big do you think his dreams could be?

Perhaps we'll see.

He soared his yard the whole day through.

A pilot who leads a skilled flight crew.

He cared for plants and
animals too.

An ecologist.

Maybe he'll run the zoo!

He could whip up a meal,

delicious with love.

A gourmet chef,

or something thereof.

He protected his friends.

The law, not above.

An officer's badge would fit like a glove.

Break down machines and put them together.

Create new things to make the world better!

He graphs the rain.

The snow he

measures.

He may just learn to

predict the weather

He explores the park as if it were space.

He'll help us win the next space race.

He stands with poise and speaks with respect.

He may become president-elect.

He counted the bees, and numbers were low.

He knows they're needed for food to grow.

Beekeeper or farmer, maybe he'll be.

He'll change the world. He has the key.

A Musician.

Maybe he'll learn the

tuba,

or save our reefs by

learning to scuba.

Skip the tuba and

lead the band.

The orchestra's

tempo is in his hands.

He crosses the pond and nurtures the ducks.

Success isn't always just wearing a tux.

He could cross the sea, and where would he be?

In Haiti, where he could help those in need.

He teaches of kindness. He is a good person.

He won't stand by and watch the world worsen.

The fruit of the spirit flows from his heart.

He'll better the world, even if in small part.

There was a brown boy, and he had big dreams!

It's all up to him to decide what to be.

How big do you think his dreams could be?

Perhaps we'll see.

AIR TRAFFIC CONTROLLER · ANIMAL TRAINER
ARCHITECT · ASTRONAUT · ASTRONOMER
AUTHOR · BIOLOGIST · BOTANIST
BUSINESS OWNER · CHEMIST · COACH · DENTIST
DESIGNER · DIRECTOR · ECOLOGIST · ECONOMIST
EDUCATOR · ENGINEER · FINANCIAL ADVISOR
FIREFIGHTER · GEOLOGIST · GRAPHIC DESIGNER
HORTICULTURIST · IMMUNOLOGIST
INTERPRETER · INVESTOR · IT PROFESSIONAL
JEWELER · JOURNALIST · JUDGE · LAWYER
LIBRARIAN · METEOROLOGIST · MUSICIAN
NURSE · OCCUPATIONAL THERAPIST
OPTOMETRIST · PALEONTOLOGIST · PARK RANGER
PEDIATRICIAN · PERSONAL TRAINER
PHYSICAL THERAPIST · PILOT · POLICE OFFICER
PRESIDENT · PRINCIPAL · PRODUCER · PROFESSOR
PROGRAMMER · RADIOLOGIST · REALTOR
REPORTER · SCIENTIST · SPEECH THERAPIST
STATISTICIAN · SURGEON · TECHNICIAN
TRANSLATOR · VETERINARIAN
VIDEOGRAPHER · VIROLOGIST · WEB DESIGNER
WRITER · ZOOLOGIST

I DREAM OF BECOMING A . . .

Age 5 _____

Age 6 _____

Age 7 _____

Age 8 _____

Age 9 _____

Age 10 _____

Age 11 _____

Age 12 _____

CPSIA information can be obtained
at www.ICGtesting.com
Printed in the USA
LVHW072149050221
677866LV00031B/87